FAVOR

THE OVERLOOKED INGREDIENT FOR SUCCESS

Rhoda Banks

5 Fold Media
visit us at www.5foldmedia.com

Favor
Copyright © 2010 by Rhoda Banks

Published by 5 Fold Media, LLC
www.5foldmedia.com

All rights reserved. No part of this book may be reproduced, stored in a retrieval system, or transmitted in any form or by any means-electronic, mechanical, photocopy, recording, or otherwise-without prior written permission of the copyright owner, except by a reviewer who wishes to quote brief passages in connection with a review for inclusion in a magazine, website, newspaper, podcast, or broadcast.

Unless otherwise indicated, Scripture quoted by permission. Quotations designated (NIV) are from THE HOLY BIBLE: NEW INTERNATIONAL VERSION®. NIV®. Copyright © 1973, 1978, 1984 by International Bible Society. Used by permission of Zondervan Publishing House. All rights reserved."

"Scripture taken from the NEW AMERICAN STANDARD BIBLE®, Copyright © 1960,1 962,1963,1968,1971,1972,1973,1975,1977,1995 by The Lockman Foundation. Used by permission."

"Scripture quotations taken from the Amplified® Bible,
Copyright © 1954, 1958, 1962, 1964, 1965, 1987 by The Lockman Foundation. Used by permission." (www.Lockman.org)

ISBN:978-0-9827980-1-0

Cover design by Cathy Sanders @ 5 Fold Media

Acknowledgments

I give thanks and honor to my Lord Jesus Christ for His divine authorship of this project.

Also I give special acknowledgment to my Pastor, Dr. Phil Gauthier, for his wisdom and insight, helping this book come to life and giving it balance. I also want to thank Pastor Carolyn for her support and giving nature.

Thanks to Kathy Lombardi for giving me encouragement and inspiration, and spurring me on to achieve more.

I also want to thank my mentors at the Christian Writer's Guild, Di Ann Mills and Stephen, and Janet Bly who gave me the impetus to keep writing and not give up.

And lastly, my husband Brian who believed that this project could become a book.

Thanks to Pastor Tony Kober of New Life Church in Patterson, NY, for his dedication to the Gospel, and instruction in my life. You are a blessing.

Also I would like to thank Pastor Lizzie Louis for her friendship and for inspiring me to dream big dreams.

Endorsements

At a time when so many are concerned about prospering, Rhoda Banks offers wisdom and strategy to access, understand, and walk out the abundant life promised in the Scriptures. Rhoda's prophetic insight and teaching provides the reader with the necessary elements to experience the divine favor of the Lord.

This book is a clarion call to all who desire true success, to seek God's best on His terms.

Come to the banquet table and allow this prophetic teacher to counsel you with wisdom and revelation; poured out from the mind of God on how to be aided, preferred, and supported by God's favor beyond your wildest dreams.

Pastor Lizzie Louis, MPA, MA
Sweet Deliverance Ministries/Pouring the Oil

Favor is a gift from God that is ours through faith in Jesus Christ. Rhoda Banks offers insight into how a believer can receive and walk in the favor of God. May those who read this book receive encouragement as they continue to grow and walk in the favor of God.

Dr. Phil Gauthier
Pastor of Hope in Life Church, Carmel, New York

Contents

Chapter	Page
Introduction	1
1. What Brings Favor Into a Person's Life?	5
2. Wisdom and Understanding	9
3. Kingdom Thinking: Having the Mind of Christ	13
4. Praise and Worship	17
5. Staying in the Love of God	21
6. How to Walk in Favor	23
Endnotes	26
Bibliography	27

Introduction

Favor is the essential element toward advancement in this world. Many people try to gain favor, but it's often elusive. Without favor, it's hard to get what we want, and even harder to convince other people that we are credible. We need a blueprint or plan on how to increase favor in our lives. As we allow the favor of God to bring us into a place of prominence, we begin to break through areas that were previously locked.

Lance Wallnau, a Pastor in Rhode Island, states that "Favor is the special affection of God toward you that releases an influence on you, so that others are inclined to like you, or to cooperate with you." He says that FAVOR is like being dipped in honey so that the blessings of God stick to us. [1]

Favor means to aid, prefer, or support. One of the meanings which I really like is to bend (condescend), or stoop in kindness to an inferior. In the New Testament, *favor* comes from the Greek word: "Charis." This is where we get our word for Grace. It is where we get our wording for the gifts of the Holy Spirit, or charismata gifts. Listen, even the gifts of the Holy Spirit are a sign of God's favor on us. [2]

Although grace and favor come from the same root word, they are different. Grace is undeserved, while there are conditions to engender the favor of God. In other words, there are measures we can take to ensure we walk in God's favor.

Psalm 84:11 states, "For the Lord God is a sun and Shield, the Lord bestows (present) grace and favor and (future) glory (honor, splendor, and heavenly bliss)! No good thing will He withhold from those who walk uprightly" (Amplified).

We are developing character when we allow our desires to be controlled by the Holy Spirit and we follow His dictates. As we receive God's direction and obey it, then we are enabled to move into a place of great favor. In turn this gives us great confidence, allowing us to bring God great glory. We are told not to cast away our confidence, because it has great reward, and after we have done the will of God we will receive what's been promised (see Hebrews 10:35). I believe that one of these rewards is having the favor of God.

Favor comes when the will of God is realized. When we allow the Lord to tame our desires and to put away unwholesome habits and speech, then we are able to enter into a whole new dimension of His power and authority.

We need to understand that while grace is undeserved, it is not cheap or easily bought. We must step into a place where we allow God's working to change us, and then we can move into all that He has destined for us. We are being taken from glory to glory. Favor is required.

My pastor, Dr. Phil Gauthier of Hope in Life Church in Carmel, New York, recently was talking to me about this subject. He mentioned that favor must still be received and acted on by faith. One can frustrate the grace of God.

He went on to explain that we already have God's favor in Christ. We are fully favored when we are born again, because we are His very own loved children. However, we must appropriate God's favor through faith, and also walk according to the truths presented in this book.

My sincere wish is that all that read this book receive encouragement and hope to walk out their divine destiny. May you gain understanding and wisdom that enables you to reach for the high calling of the Lord Jesus Christ.

Chapter 1
What Brings Favor Into a Person's Life?

Patient Endurance in Adversity
Standing the Test, Waiting, and Surrender

As a person is able to stand up under the winds of adversity and maintain their faith, it releases God's hand of favor in their life. As a person develops a preserving spirit, they are enabled to bring great glory to the Lord. So, it takes a person who is willing to endure hardship in an effort to advance the kingdom that brings a release of God's blessing. For as we live to please Him, and we count it all joy, we are taken to a place of supernatural blessing, because He calls them blessed who endure.

So, when we keep the faith in the midst of trying circumstances, we are showing that we really trust the Lord, and that we are not going by what we see, but by faith. The just shall live by faith (see Hebrews 10:38).

The Lord is able to trust a person who is willing to see the outcome of their faith, because they have stood the test. When a person stands testing, they are rewarded with many crowns. One of the benefits of testing is the favor that comes afterward. It's a reward for standing firm and not losing hope. It's the will of God to bless you and to bless people through you.

Once a person passes the test, they are enabled to be taken to a new level. New levels require greater wisdom and knowledge. But before higher levels of leadership can be given, it is necessary for the individual to be broken. "For everyone to whom much is given, of him shall much be required" (Luke 12:48, Amplified).

An example of being broken to receive favor can be seen in the life of Joseph. Although Joseph saw glimpses of favor in his life (the coat of many colors, the dream of his brothers bowing down to him, and the favor he received from Potiphar while in jail), he did not enter into the fullness of favor until he became second in command to Pharaoh. He endured constant hardship until God used Joseph's ability to interpret dreams to save his masses of people and even his family from the famine. He had to wait until God lifted him up at the proper time.

"For this finds favor, if for the sake of conscience toward God a man bears up under sorrows when suffering unjustly. For what credit is there, if when you sin and are harshly treated, you endure it with patience? But if when you do what is right, and suffer for it patiently endure it, this finds favor with God" (1 Peter 2:19-20, NASB).

Doing what is right; staying under the hand of God and entrusting yourself to Him, speaks of a life of faith. Testing comes before promotion, but preparation is never wasted.

The full measure of favor in Joseph's life did not manifest until he entered into his destiny. At this point he was able to handle it, because of his reliance on the Lord. From Joseph's life we see that favor is not given completely at one time, it is progressive.

A modern day example of this can be seen in Susan Boyle. She looked pretty ordinary the day she auditioned on the British Version of American Idol in 2009. Little did the world know that she had been preparing for this day all her life. She had been practicing her singing with little notoriety, yet all it took was the right moment, and her dream became a reality. She became an overnight sensation, which released such favor that the song, *I Dreamed a Dream* went gold.[3]

God uses the weak things of this world to confound the wise. He does his best work through vessels that allow life's circumstances to shape and mold them into His image. It takes a willing heart that allows Him to bring correction, forfeiting what appears to be His will, in favor of losing your life. It takes a consecrated heart to leave behind all that hinders our walk, but as you lose your life, you find that you are walking in a new dimension of the Spirit. Pruning is never easy, but once you bring your desires under the control of the Holy Spirit, then you are moved into a place of promise. It's not about how you can serve the Lord, but how you can become a vessel who is able to contain and carry the glory of God. It comes when you count it all joy and give up your own will in favor of His will.

Chapter 2
Wisdom and Understanding

Prayer, Heeding Correction, Being Kind, Speaking the Truth, Obedience

Proverbs 24:3-4 states, "By wisdom a house is built, and through understanding it is established; through knowledge its rooms are filled with rare and beautiful treasures."

The way we seek wisdom is by being taught. We allow the Word to have its way in our lives. It is not seeking knowledge for the sake of knowledge, but it goes beyond that. We allow God's Word to have an affect on our behavior. We gain insight by seeking Him, and asking Him to remove that which is displeasing.

It's revelation knowledge that causes the light bulb to go on. Once we gain understanding, then we must act on it. Favor will manifest blessings.

Having a relationship with the Lord where we learn to listen is vitally important to advance. Sometimes, we must travail in prayer to break through barriers and to have other people also praying (to intercede) for us. We need to get a hold of His garment and not let go until we gain the wisdom of God for our situation. The prayer of agreement is very powerful in this regard.

David inquired of the Lord before going into battle, which brought him much favor. By doing this, David was able to gain strategy and win many battles.

Daniel was a man of wisdom. He not only was a trusted advisor of the king, but also a man of prayer. His ability to interpret dreams brought him favor.

Even though he got thrown in the lion's den, God shut the mouth of the lions because of Daniel's faithfulness in seeking Him. Thus God uses the abilities and gifts that He gives us to bring favor. One, who is skillful in his work, will go before kings. The Bible says your gift will make room for you (Proverbs 18:16).

Having wisdom opens many doors. We see in the life of Solomon, that when he asked for wisdom, God also gave him riches. When we know how to apply what God has given us, through understanding we prosper. However, when we live to please ourselves, rather than God, we fall.

In the book of Proverbs, there are many verses about heeding correction, and how it brings honor and favor. Proverbs 13:18 states, "He who ignores discipline comes to poverty and shame, but whoever heeds correction is honored."

Proverbs 13:15 says, "Good understanding wins favor, but the way of the unfaithful is hard."

Our words are a measure of our heart condition. We must use our words wisely, for God values truth. He wants us to speak the truth in love. God delights when we learn how to use our tongues to bless and encourage others, rather than use destructive language. We are walking in wisdom when we adhere to God's statues, and really believe Him.

"My son, do not forget my teaching, but keep my commands in your heart, for they will prolong your life many years and bring you prosperity. Let love and faithfulness never leave you; bind them around your neck, write them on the tablet of your heart. Then you will win favor and a good name in the sight of God and man." (Proverbs 3 1-4).

Chapter 3
Kingdom Thinking: Having the Mind of Christ

Being Filled With the Spirit, Having the Spirit of an Overcomer

Pastor Jerry Vargo at Sermon Central on the Internet did a series on walking in the favor of God. He lists three things needed to walk in your dreams.
1. Total unconditional surrender
2. Absolute purity
3. Kingdom thinking: having the mind of Christ

He says that all these things produce favor [4]

While I have touched upon the first two in some detail, I want to focus on having a kingdom mentality.

When you have a kingdom mentality, you look for ways to advance the kingdom. You are always learning and have a humble attitude. You become a visionary and seek to do things God's way.

When we allow His kingdom to be formed in us, we keep ourselves filled with the Spirit. This enables us to keep the fire burning on the altar. As we determine to keep the fire lit, we are enabled to do exploits in His name.

Praying in the Spirit enables us to pray God's perfect will into the circumstance. This allows His will to be accomplished. This is a birthing process which allows His kingdom purposes to come into fruition.

David was a kingdom thinker. He had a heart after God, and even though he failed, he had a passion to see God's kingdom expand. He wanted to build a temple for the Lord, but it was his son Solomon whom God commissioned to do it.

Noah also had God's favor when He asked him to build an ark. Noah did everything in accordance with God's specifications. Even when others laughed and mocked him, he persisted in going forth with God's plan and purpose.

Jesus had a strong desire to complete His destiny. This is what kept His focus, even in the midst of suffering. Completing the course laid out for Him on the cross brought the full package of favor, deliverance, and freedom.

The spirit of an overcomer is marked by remaining steadfast in your faith, even in the midst of suffering. To accomplish this we must stay filled with God's Spirit, and rely on His promises in the storms of life. We must keep ourselves listening for His voice, to fortify our defenses. It brings a blessing into your life when you allow God's Spirit to move in your circumstance. It takes a concerted effort to keep oneself from straying off the path, but as we keep our eyes fixed on the prize of the high calling, we will reap the benefits of holy living. He is a rewarder of those who diligently seek Him (see Hebrews 11:6).

When our minds are readied for increase, then we are able to secure more territory for the kingdom. It takes a certain boldness to bring it about, but as we determine to stay filled with His

Spirit and to praise Him daily, then we come into a place of supernatural increase.

The Lord tells us to desire the greater gifts, especially prophecy. In other words, he wants us to increase and do greater works.

An example of this can be seen when I first found out I had the gift of prophecy. In the beginning I was only able to receive the prophecy in written form. This was in the year 2000.

So, I went to a prophecy class in 2006, at Gateway Christian Fellowship with Prophet Dennis Cramer. Everyone, with the exception of myself and one other person, got up and just prophesied over others in the class out loud, without paper. I did not feel led to do this, nor did I think I could.

But the morning of July 7th, 2007, everything changed. I praised the Lord, and he told me that I would have the increase. So, on 7/7/07, I began to prophecy out loud spontaneously. (This completes a 7 year cycle.)

Here I thought maybe I didn't have the faith to prophecy, but it's God who brings the increase. All I needed to do was ask and praise him with expectancy that he can do exceedingly, more than I could think or ask (see Ephesians 3:20).

Chapter 4
Praise and Worship

Giving, Unity, Thankfulness

Praise allows the peace of God to descend over the circumstances at hand. It brings God the glory and He is magnified through the worship. God inhabits the praises of His people. Praise is a powerful weapon of spiritual warfare. Praise breaks open areas of demonic interference and removes blockages that keep a person in bondage.

For example, David would play the harp for Saul (who was tormented by an evil spirit). When he would play the harp, the spirit would depart, and Saul felt better.

David had a heart of worship, which helped to encourage himself in tough times. As a worshipper and intercessor, God's anointing rested on David because his heart was bent on seeking God. Those who know their God will be strong and do exploits (see Daniel 11:32). David won many battles because he depended on the Lord for strategy and victory. His favor came from his heart attitude. Worship reflected his heart and passion for the Lord.

We need to praise Him in the dark places. For when we do, a release of God's power manifests.

What we have heard in the dark, we need to proclaim in the light.

When Paul and Silas were in the jail, bound up and beaten, they began to praise the Lord at the midnight hour. As a result, an earthquake erupted, which set them free, and resulted in the jailer getting saved. Matthew 11:12 states, " From the days of John the Baptist until now, the kingdom of heaven has been forcefully advancing, and forceful men lay hold of it."

Another way we give thanks to God is through our giving. When we give _sacrificially_, we show our dependence on Him. God is pleased when we exercise our faith! We offer up the sacrifice of praise, to offset the spirit of heaviness. We have to keep ourselves filled with the Spirit, singing spiritual songs, so we can be houses of praise, that ushers His presence into the atmosphere. We have to rise up and use the weapon of praise to make a way through the wilderness.

The Israelites would send the singers into battle first, because they knew that God would be with them. God's presence brings the anointing, and the anointing breaks the yoke of bondage.

I had a dream that I was in a haunted castle, a few years ago. In the dream I began to hear demonic voices and I started to bind the voices and tell them to "GO"! The voices got quieter, but they were still there. As I began praising and thanking the Lord, the voices left and the heaviness was gone. The whole atmosphere changed and became light and airy.

When we use our spiritual weapons (the full armor of God, praise and worship etc), we dispel doubt and build our faith. We show that we are keeping ourselves in the love of God as we seek Him in all His glory.

When we praise Him in unity, God's power is released. When the disciples were in the upper room, and in one accord, they began speaking with tongues of fire. Unity, giving and worship all work together. When the spirit of peace is maintained, God can move unhindered. Peace is the potting soil of revelation, and after revelation, manifestation appears.

Chapter 5
Staying in the Love of God

Encouragement, Forgiveness

Love is the force that binds everything together. Without it, we are walking in the flesh, and no one will notice God in us. When we fully comprehend God's love for us, we are then able to love others. We seek to look for good and be an encouragement.

Without love, we can be gifted without measure, but still not be effective. There is nothing special in ourselves alone that sets us apart from others. To be a city on a hill and to stand out, we need to shine for Christ. If we are holding grudges, talking about others, and refusing to forgive, we can't be a witness. The world must see something different; we must be people of integrity.

To forgive offenses, we must allow the healing oil of the Holy Spirit to minister to us, but we must also be able to speak the truth in love. How we approach others often determines their response. That's why the Bible says to overcome evil with good.

God's kind of love is full of mercy and grace. That's why when we walk in love; we are walking in the Spirit. We are displaying the fruit of the Spirit. For it takes a concerted effort to keep ourselves in the love of God, but as we seek peaceful relations, we are able to stay focused and remain calm. When Joseph forgave his brothers, he was displaying God's kind of love.

As we seek to keep ourselves filled with God's presence, we are enabled to bring Him great glory. This brings a refreshing. We are seeking Him on a whole new level when we keep ourselves flowing in His Spirit, and allow His Spirit to change our mindset. We keep ourselves filled with the Spirit, so we can receive a fresh outpouring that enables us to love.

To walk in love, we must be on guard against the little foxes that try to steal our joy. In His presence is fullness of joy (see Psalm 16:11). We must remain vigilant and keep coming to the feet of Jesus when circumstances come to try and take the joy of the Lord from us. When we understand the price He paid, then we are enabled to bring Him glory by the way we live. As we do these things, we can be assured that God will recompense us, and give us favor.

Chapter 6
How to Walk in Favor

Practical Applications

When we develop a kingdom mindset, we are positioned for victory. We need to think thoughts that are consistent with His plans for our lives to see them come to pass. When we allow His thoughts to become our thoughts, then we progress.

"Delight yourself in the Lord and He will give you the desires of your heart" (Psalm 37:4).

When we allow His desires to become our desires we find favor in His eyes. We are not our own, we must make wise choices. In order to do this, we must renew our minds to His word and act on it.

We must be diligent to keep our affections from straying. Distractions, trials and all kinds of circumstances come to rob us of our peace, but as we contend for the faith and stay connected to the Bible, we are able to stay focused on our goals.

There must be a determination to pray in the Spirit on all occasions, and to speak to the mountains in our lives. We have to stay prayed up knowing that the enemy of our souls is trying to find ways to destroy us. Because of this, we must be fully armed. We come into a place of favor as we resist the enemy's plans for our lives and live to please God.

We are developing His character when we leave behind the hindrances and stay under His hand. In order to do this we must be led by the Holy Spirit and ask Him to reveal what the hindrances are.

As we take our place in the Spirit realm we are enabled to do what we are set apart to do. We have a call on our lives, but it can be missed if we live to please our fleshly desires. So, we must remain convinced that He is able to bring us into a place of fulfillment. As we call the things that are not as though they are, we are speaking into existence the things that are not yet fulfilled.

We need to decree that we have favor beforehand and thank Him for it. We speak the Scriptures over ourselves and make it personal. We can battle in the Spirit with what we speak over our situations. We need to war over our prophecies and decree them into existence.

I believe favor comes from exercising our faith and relying on His promises. When we maintain the attitude of an overcomer, it brings us into a place of favor. It is time to stop relying on outdated methods and to keep oneself filled with the Spirit. As you rely on your own understanding, it keeps you from fulfilling what God has in store for you. It's not about what you can do on your own, but about what He will do through you. Favor is a gift from God that allows you to move ahead. Without His presence and wisdom we can do nothing. Our desire to move ahead does not matter as much as His call on our lives, and what He desires. It is imperative to keep our eyes on the prize, so we can advance in His calling on our lives.

In conclusion, as we remain patient and endure through the testing of our faith, we will gain favor if we don't give up. We have to believe that we serve a God of restoration who is working to see us come into a place of increase and favor. As we stay filled with His Spirit, we come into a place where we are changed, and as we are changed, we mount up with wings as eagles and soar with the glory of God shining through us, and a crown of favor as our reward.

Endnotes

1. Jerry Vargo, Walking in the Favor of the Lord- Part 3. Sermon Central, December 2003. pg. 2.

2. Jerry Vargo, Walking in the Favor of the Lord- Part 1. Sermon Central, November 2003. pg. 2.

3. For more information about Susan Boyle's story, see http://en.wikipedia.org/wiki/Susan_Boyle.

4. Jerry Vargo, Walking in the Favor of the Lord- Part 1. Sermon Central, November 2003. pg. 2.

Bibliography

Pastor Jerry Vargo, Walking in the Favor of the Lord- Sermon Central, Part 1-4, November 2003-January 2004.

Wikipedia; the Free Encyclopedia. "Susan Boyle." http://en.wikipedia.org/wiki/Susan_Boyle. (Accessed July, 2010).

About the Author

After graduating from Columbia University in New York in 1987, Rhoda Banks worked as a clinical social worker with the chronically mentally ill population in New York State, before entering into private practice.

As a Christian counselor for over 12 years, she has helped many people not only heal emotionally, but grow in their faith. Her passion led her to start Recovery Ministries, a ministry designed to help the hurting and minister to God's people in the midst of the storm. She also holds a Marriage Tune-up Group in the community to strengthen communication and conflict management skills.

Rhoda has been a keynote speaker for Women's Aglow and has written published articles for The Wise Counsel Guide.

Currently, she is involved in prophetic ministry at Hope in Life Church in Carmel, New York and is attending Bible school there. Her vision is to see the body of Christ built up and functioning in a healthy way. She desires for the bride to come into the fullness that Christ designed even before the foundation of the world.

Rhoda is available for speaking or teaching engagements and can be reached at rhodabanks@att.net.

5 Fold Media, LLC is a Spirit-led, for-profit media company. Our desire is to produce lasting fruit in writing, music, art, and creative gifts.

Get your book published!

**For more information visit:
www.5foldmedia.com**